Business Impact Selling

A Margin Growth Opportunity

"How to outsmart your competition by extending the language of selling from price, features and benefits to business impact discussions"

THOUGHTS FROM THE FIELD

"The best sales training of my entire 18-year sales career. When your eyes are opened to the fact that selling should be about delivering tangible business outcomes for customers it raises your game and you recognize that what you are doing is driving your customer's growth, market share and margin which in turn drives wider economic growth. That, in turn, gives you greater gravitas and job satisfaction."

Chris Cappello
Director of Sales-Mid Atlantic at Comport Consulting

PREFACE

In today's hyper-competitive and rapidly changing marketplace, sales organizations and salespeople are being increasingly challenged to demonstrate they have both the understanding and the ability to provide measurable "business impact" services and solutions that strongly align to the customers business goals and strategy.

This is the type of "transformation" that Exceed helps sales organisations to be able to execute in every client engagement.

Business Impact selling is more than a book, a speaker, a seminar, or this year's management theme. Many people think they know what it is, but in most cases, they fail to understand the depth of this business philosophy and sales process. Business Impact focused salespeople take the initiative to add value. These salespeople do not wait for the customer to complain about the price and then start outlining their value. They build more value in on the front end so that price becomes less of an issue on the back end.

Because of this customer value focus, business impact salespeople are in business to make a difference, not just to make a deal. They approach the sale by asking themselves this question, "Where can we have the greatest impact on the customer's business?" It is a process of identifying viable opportunities, penetrating these accounts thoroughly, qualifying these opportunities, capturing the business, assuring buyer satisfaction, and retaining and growing the business. The latter activities differentiate business impact selling from traditional selling.

In traditional selling, salespeople focus on offensive selling activities; i.e. pursuing new business. In fact, there is a bad case of pipeline-itis across the globe.

Managers are so obsessed with finding new business and discovering new opportunities that they often ignore their existing customers.

It's ensuring you shut your back door so that you don't lose as much business from the back door as you bring in the front door. A big part of what business impact salespeople do is to assure customer satisfaction with what they've sold the customer. They follow up. During this follow up they discover additional opportunities for business. For one-tenth the cost of acquiring new business, you can service an existing account and grow the business.

Initially, the impact-added salesperson is a diagnostician—he or she diagnoses the customer's problems and then prescribes the right solution. The salesperson evolves into the promoter or persuader mode. It's here that the business impact salesperson positions his company as the value-add supplier, differentiates his solution, and presents his offering in a compelling business focused language.

Business impact selling is significantly different than traditional selling. Traditional salespeople sell products—business impact salespeople solve problems. Traditional salespeople make deals—business impact salespeople want to make a difference. The fundamental selling skill for traditional salespeople is closing—the fundamental selling skill for value focused salespeople is probing and listening.

Bottom Line? Add value, not cost. Sell value, not price!

The Traditional Sales Approach	What's Needed?
• Respond to what the customer asks for • Position features and benefits with little focus on selling business outcomes • High levels of price negotiation • Sell within comfort zone • Focus on IT customer base and avoid LOB customers • Attend many unproductive meetings driving cost of sale • Low accountability • Low forecasting accuracy • Lack of healthy and disciplined sales best practice • Erratic win:planning • Lack of quality and tracked key account growth planning • Low level of negotiation skills	• Focus on delivering clear and tangible business outcomes not just IT ones • Move the concept of selling to recognize the sales PROFESSION is about showing customers how to make money, save money, reduce risk or all three • Utilize sales best practices for every customer meeting, sales opportunity and key account relationships. High forecasting accuracy • Constantly seeking to embrace new technologies and continually grow skills (operates at the unconscious competent not unconscious incompetent level) • Sells in an intentional manner, never skates • Always hunting for new opportunities to bring value to customer table

Chapter 1

So, when you were asked, at the ripe old age of 7 or 8, what you'd like to be when you grew up, did you answer, "salesperson"?   Maybe you did, maybe you didn't. Regardless of that answer, this book sets out some of the key fundamentals of effective, professional selling; this, for some of you, will merely be a sharpening of the sword and, for others, a great introduction to the world of professional business impact selling.   Solid, common sense ideas to drive you toward business success.

As a salesperson, the first thing to get inside your head is that selling is arguably one of the most important professions in the world and a job to be immensely proud of – so long as you are selling the business outcomes of your solutions or services.   Until someone sells something, there is little need for any of the other groups and divisions that constitute a successful company.   As salespeople, operating in any economic climate – challenging or otherwise – the importance of adopting a sales approach focused on delivering quantified business impact is critical for developing long-term customer loyalty and extension business.

Customers examine every major investment avenue there is to ensure that they produce significant business impact.   In simpler terms, selling is about helping customers *make money, save money, or both.*   All other results end in the same thing as well – making or saving money.   If you recognize that your job is about creating tangible value for customers, which, in turn, drives the overall economy, you'll soon begin to see just how important and proud you should be of your role, not to forget the increased commission this will bring!

Regardless of how long you've been selling, you'll recognize the importance of staying at the top of your game. The best always wants to be better; for you, this book may just be a sharpening of the sword. For others – those who are new to selling or have only a few months of experience – these chapters will provide you with the foundation of good professional selling. As with any other skill, it is the foundation of good skills that distinguishes the average, good, and world-class performers. Just think about that in the context of the best sports personalities – they just make the basics look easy but that comes from daily practice routines to perfect those basics!

This book will refresh your memory of or introduce you to the skills and best practices in sales that permanently transform your sales approach to one that is firmly focused on delivering significant business benefits, that is, helping customers drive cost down or drive revenue up. Or both. If you are already selling on value, well done! This program will serve as a refresher of the skills and techniques required to stay on top of your selling activities.

C-level customers continue to invest but only where there are clear and tangible reasons to do so. Our job, as salespeople, must be to focus on delivering propositions that will help customers drive and exceed their business objectives.

Without a strong business case supporting the investment,

you'll most likely face delays in closing deals and a heavy emphasis on the "sharpen your pencil" discount requests.

While many of the skills and techniques outlined in this book are applicable to all salespeople, the target audiences are those selling high-value solutions and services to businesses in every sector be that on the phone or face-to-face

Chapter 2

Selling, nowadays, is much greater than simply responding to what a customer says he/she wants. It's more about delivering the best advice possible. It's about being able to diagnose the customer's real needs and proactively offer innovative ideas to the customer to demonstrate how your services or products can help them *make money or save money* – long before even they consider them. Selling in such a proactive manner will set you apart from other salespeople, and this book will provide you with the skills and sales techniques necessary to operate in today's demanding business climate.

Take a look at illustration 1.

5	Contribute to Business Strategy
4	**Deliver Quantifiable Business Value**
3	Deliver comprehensive product & extensive service & support
2	Deliver product and some services
1	Deliver product

In levels 1-3 you sell what the customer WANTS
In levels 4 and 5 you are selling what the customer NEEDS

Think of any customer and ask yourself, where would they place you today in terms of the business relationship with your organization. Would they describe the relationship as being purely a product one, in other words, at level 1? Or would they say that you are delivering more than just that – good service and great products? That would be a level 2 relationship. Level 3 suggests that you are going further by delivering services, support, and perhaps some consultancy. The relationship is, therefore, much stronger.

Level 4 describes a relationship where the customer sees the quantified business value you are providing. And level 5 describes a relationship where you are assisting in defining the business strategy (level 5 is where company corporate advisors are placed in terms of mergers, acquisitions etc.)

Price, features, and competition are much more prevalent when you are selling at the lower levels, and you are more vulnerable to attack. As you move up the levels, these things become less important, since you're recognized for delivering quantified business value.

Wherever you are today, the question remains: How do you climb higher, or if you are already at level 4, how do you remain there?

According to a recent study pertaining to technology buyers, the most cited reason for changing vendors is not that the new provider had a vastly superior technology or delivered thought leadership in a changing business landscape. It is most significantly because the challenger offered a **SOLID BUSINESS CASE FOR CHANGE.**

This business case quantifies how the new vendor can deliver superior business benefits (improved productivity and processes, reduced risks and revenue gains) while simultaneously lowering the total cost of ownership compared to the current vendor.

According to a research by UBM Tech, the top factors that led to a change of vendors included the following:

- **42%** – Case for Change, where the new vendor demonstrated a business case for change

- **41%** – Unrealized ROI, where the existing vendor did not deliver the knowledge or training to realize the value in the solution

- **38%** – Superior Knowledge, where the new vendor demonstrated a better understanding of the customer's company and industry

- **27%** – Thought Leadership, where the market research demonstrated a change in business landscape

The Bottom Line

If you are the incumbent, in order to maintain account loyalty, you need to assure your customers they are achieving the expected value, as **41%** of the participants in the study indicated that they switched not because of anything the challenger did but because the incumbent failed to prove realized ROI.

If you are the challenger, in **almost half** of the cases where a change occurred, it was the business case that made all the difference.

Delivering tangible business value means being able to demonstrate the economic impact of your product or solution on the customer's business. In the world of Information Technology, that means translating technological benefits into business benefits. It's all too easy to talk about greater reliability, flexibility, scalability, and improved productivity from IT investments, but what does that translate to in terms of driving increased revenue, reducing operating and capital expenditure, reducing risk, or all three? The process needs to begin with a clear understanding of your customer's business strategy, goals, objectives, and challenges. The best way to kick-start that is to conduct your own research.

The majority of public and private organizations have a web-site crammed full of information, all of which can provide hints regarding their strategy, priorities, and challenges. Hints that can then serve as a catalyst for business discussions that lead to opportunities for you to position the value of your solution linked to their plans.

In a recent meeting between an HPE partner and a CIO as one of his prospects, the CIO ended the meeting by thanking the salesperson for not mentioning one product in the entire span of the 60-minute meeting. The salesperson had successfully taken his time to conduct his research and develop his questions to better understand the customer's business. He opened the meeting by saying that his organization focused on delivering tangible value from IT investments and cited an example of how they had helped similar organizations increase the time to revenue through an improved time to service launch. In other words, he earned the right to ask his questions, having delivered a compelling reason for his customer to wish to listen to him. (There will be more on this in a later chapter.)

Let's now look at how you can underpin everything you do by being excellent at the basics of sound, professional business-value selling.

Wherever you are on the 5 levels of the "selling ladder" today, this book will help you develop or hone your skills further and sell more value to your customers, thus reducing discount levels and increasing customer loyalty.

Being excellent with the basics of selling provides you with a foundation to build on. Selling is a skill, and like any skill, you have to perfect the basics in order to excel.

Wherever you are on the road to becoming a business impact–focused sales professional, there is one thing that will set you apart in the world of selling ... Never stray from recognizing that your true role is to deliver quantified value from every investment your customer makes with you.

It's all too easy to fall into bad habits without realizing it. Think about learning to drive – you start out as an **unconscious incompetent**, you don't have a clue about how to drive, but it all looks so easy. You soon realize it isn't. You gradually move to a state of **conscious incompetence** as you recognize just how much more difficult it is to actually drive a car with confidence and skill.   As you progress, taking and passing your test, you move to a state of **conscious competence.**   For many weeks, you are thinking about every aspect of your driving.   That's the safest state to be in.   The danger arises when you move to a state of **unconscious incompetence.**   You think you know how to drive and maybe start to forget some of the essential safety rules.   That's when accidents happen.

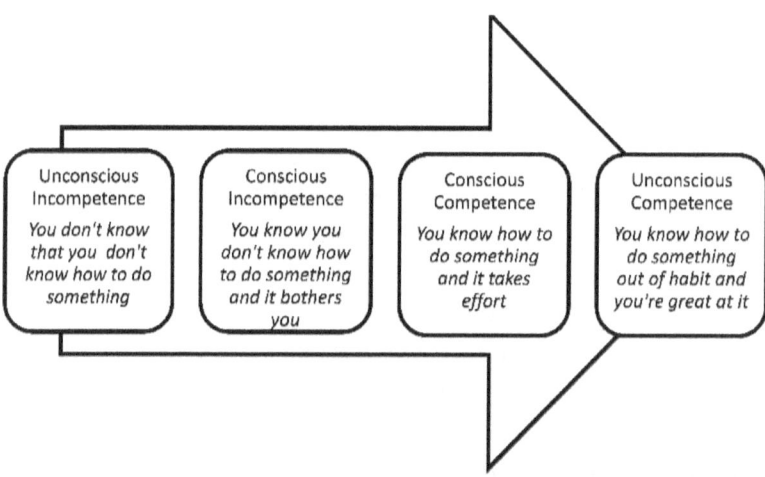

Since selling is a skill you need in order to be on top of your game each and every day, focus on practicing and perfecting the fundamental techniques of the profession in a consciously competent state of mind.   In other words, get these techniques into "muscle memory".   We've asked thousands of salespeople if they think selling is an ART or SCIENCE. Many tell us it's an ART, but the more experienced admit it's both.   It's a science because there are tried and tested techniques and skills that set you apart from your competitors.   You just have to make it look like an ART the same way top tennis players, golfers, or baseball players all make it look like an easy art.

So, let's start by looking at some of the skills we need in order to develop customer relationships to Level 4 and beyond ... and then keep them there! We'll begin with a quick reminder on the need to ensure that every single selling minute is put to good use.

Our research suggests that the average cost of conducting a face-to-face sales meeting with a customer can be in the excess of US$1500. For the purpose of this example, we are assuming an average meeting time of 1.5 hours with an hour on either end for travelling.

We then interviewed 2500 customers in middle management positions, asking the following question:

> "When salespeople come to see you, what do you think of the relative progress which is made in those meeting?"

The analysis of the results showed that 80% or 4 out of every 5 meetings make "little," "no," or "negative" progress in the customers' opinion.

So, what are the reasons they provided for this negligible progress?

One is the lack of preparation and planning and a lack of focus on the customer's business needs.   Plus, they need to listen more and talk less!   This last point is cited more than any other as the greatest "sin" of salespeople.

So, what can we do to ensure we make the maximum use of our selling time?

Well, before we answer that, let's just remind ourselves how precious that time really is.

Given an average work week of around 40 hours, the time spent actively selling is no more than 20% or around 8 hours. That's because so much of the time is spent on administration, deal chasing, travelling, internal meetings, conference calls, webinars, and so on.

Consider your win-to-loss ratio – the proportion of deals you work on but don't close – and assume that's running at 1:4. We have approximately 2 to 3 hours a week dedicated to effective selling time.

So, how do you ensure that every second is being put to the best use for you and your customer?

Chapter 3

It's all too easy to go from meeting to meeting without carefully planning them every step of the way. Remember, the primary focus is on establishing the customer's business needs first, so we are in a position to build the business case to demonstrate how the solution or service we are selling will help them make money, save money, or both.

Take a look at this simple but highly effective meeting plan:

(full copy at the end)

The first main section focuses on the SMART meeting OBJECTIVES.

There really is no excuse for not having an effective set of SMART objectives for every sales meeting. If there are no SMART objectives, why are you going to the meeting? Some salespeople argue that "building a relationship" is a SMART objective, but to be honest, it really isn't! There will always be some other objective that you can add into the mix!

SMART is an acronym that helps us ensure that every objective we set delivers a result. Make sure your meeting objectives are SPECIFIC – stating precisely what you need to find out and achieve. Make them MEASURABLE in order to establish progress at the end of the meeting. Try to AGREE on the objectives before the meeting and then always confirm both yours and the customers objectives at the onset.

Make them REALISTIC, so you don't try to run before you walk, and if you use the expression "By the end of the meeting, I will have …" that would make your objectives TIMEBOUND. Take a look at the following and see whether you think they fulfil the SMART criteria.

"To find information on the CRM requirement." Is this SMART or not?

No, it is not specific enough: What information is required? It is far too vague to meet the criteria!

Perhaps, something along these lines would be a little smarter:

"To establish what has prompted the need for additional capacity." It is indeed much tighter. You will certainly know whether you have accomplished this by the time you leave the meeting. It is clear and specific.

Or how about, "To identify the decision-making process by the end of the meeting"? This passes the SMART test as well. It is specific and easily measurable. You may not share this one with the customer, but it's OK to have some hidden objectives.
And this one: "To find out the business needs." It's OK but not as SMART as it can be. "To establish the top 3 business priorities for the next 6 months" may be a little SMARTer.

Just to assert your overall professionalism, don't forget to re-confirm the objectives at the beginning of every meeting. For example:

> "The key objective is to understand what has prompted the need for additional storage and servers and review how you will seek to measure the success of any investment. Once, I've understood what you are looking to achieve, I can come back with suggestions and outline the value of our proposals."

Setting and agreeing on SMART objectives help ensure that every meeting starts on a positive note.

If you really want to stand out, send a confirmation of the objectives and agenda ahead of the meeting.

> **Meeting Confirmation/Agenda**
>
> Hello John,
>
> I confirm our meeting on Tuesday, 14th March at 10.30am in your offices.
>
> We discussed the objectives for the meeting and agreed that the main area is to review your requirements to improve test time in order to reduce project delays by your 15% target.
>
> As I explained, we have extensive experience in this area and I will be pleased to discuss this with your when we meet.
>
> We agreed that I would provide you with a proposed agenda which is as follows: -
>
> i. Review of the project objectives
> ii. Determine ways in which our experience might assist in the achievement of the project goals
> iii. Agree an appropriate Action Plan
>
> If you feel that there are any other points you would like to cover please call me. I would expect the meeting to take approximately one hour and look forward to meeting you.

It shouldn't take more than a few minutes to create, but it goes a long way in establishing your professionalism before you even get to the meeting!

So, we've set the meeting up in a professional manner now. What about the reason for attending from the customer's point of view?

Chapter 4

This step revolves around the words you will use at the outset of the meeting to grasp the customer's attention from the very first second. If it's a first meeting, remember this, you don't get a second chance to make a first impression.

This technique is known as offering a **compelling business reason,** and it entails giving a statement at the outset of a meeting to attract immediate attention. You can also use it while trying to get an appointment with someone you have never met before. In fact, if you have ever tried to secure an appointment with someone (particularly someone in a senior position) and failed, it is probably due to the lack of a strong and compelling business reason for them to invest their time to meet you.

Contemplate what you can say at the start of every meeting that will make your customer or prospect sit up and take a keen interest in what you have to say. It's *the* statement that explains to the customer why they should listen to you, and that gets the meeting off to a flying start.

Let's consider a few examples – some good and some not so good.

> "Thanks for agreeing to see me today. You mentioned a need to discuss upgrades to your server infrastructure. Can I start by explaining that we have recently heard about a major new technology solution from one of our vendors, which I think would be of great benefit to your company?"

This is NOT a compelling business reason for a customer or prospect to want to hear more. It is focused on the salesperson and is heading into the "spray and pray" trap, in which you bombard the customer with product and solution overviews, hoping that something you say will resonate with them. It most probably will not. Take a look at this example:

> "I'd like to think we can focus on helping you avoid additional cost in the short term as well as looking at ways to reduce the cost and resource requirements in the long term. Can I start by asking what's prompted the need for additional systems?"

Here, the salesperson starts by focusing on the value he or she can bring to the customer's business, and that's exactly what we mean by a compelling business reason.

A Compelling Business Reason or CBR is a statement that explains to the customer "what's in it for them" to listen to you! It needs to be focused on the customer's interests, not yours.

So, let's take a look at a few more examples and include some tangible example of the potential benefits. From the customer point of view!

> "I'd like to outline a solution that can help reduce the time taken to launch your new services from 6 weeks to 1 day and help improve utilization levels by over 50%, thereby helping you to "sweat" current assets more effectively."

In this example, the focus is on what the customer may gain from the meeting – new service launches in 1 day instead of 6 weeks is a very compelling proposition for a company that depends on new service delivery. "Sweating current assets" suggests a way to reduce costs and will likely create a higher level of interest than a mere meeting to discuss the merits of a particular type of server.

In this example, the salesperson is also paying equal attention to the value he or she can offer to the customer, who is facing budget constraints.

> "... The purpose of this meeting is to demonstrate how we can offer financial services to help overcome the capital expenditure freeze and still meet your overall

Opex and Capex budget constraints ..."

In summary, a CBR provides a purpose to a meeting from the customer's point of view.

Start your planning for each and every face-to-face meeting or telephone call by having a strong set of SMART objectives – so that you can measure your progress throughout the campaign. Moreover, ensure that you are focused on understanding your customer's needs, so that you can concentrate on establishing the true business value of your solutions.

Remember the power of the COMPELLING BUSINESS REASON – it's a statement that answers the question "Why should I listen to you?" Create one for every meeting and try using the same technique for emails as well!

Chapter 5

"Bringing it all together with a powerful OPENING STATEMENT"

You don't get a second chance to make a first impression!

A good opening puts you in the best possible position to achieve your call's objectives. In order to make a good first impression, you need to get **Attention, Interest, and Involvement.** When you decide to see a movie or buy a book, you probably look at the trailer or read the blurb of the book to decide if you want to make the purchase. An opening statement is similar. It's the attention grabber to get a customer interested in what you have to say.

So, just consider what you will say to grab attention, interest and involvement in the first 90 seconds or so of each meeting. The essential ingredients for a powerful **OPENING STATEMENT** include the following:

1. Agree on the meeting objectives
2. Deliver your CBR
3. Confirm the duration
4. Agree on your **agenda** items
5. Ask an open-ended question – one that will get the customer talking

As mentioned in an earlier chapter, your agenda is a key part of the preparation and is best sent in advance. Business meetings that have no agenda are likely to have less direction and be significantly less productive than more structured meetings with a pre-set list of discussion topics. Meetings without a firm direction may stray off topic, leading to few tangible or useful results. In addition, the participants of the meeting may become disengaged if the discussion strays away from relevant topics, which can set a poor precedence for future meetings. If participants feel that meetings are unfocused and contribute little to their work, they may decide to skip future meetings.

Another important aspect of creating and circulating an agenda for business meetings ahead of time is that it offers participants an opportunity to prepare for the meeting. If the participants know the specific topics that are going to be discussed during a meeting, they can research those topics in advance and prepare the relevant information and questions to contribute constructively to the meeting. If participants know that important, relevant topics are going to be covered at meeting, they are more likely to attend it.

Remember, selling is both an art and a science!
Follow the rules of science for the selling profession but make it look like an art.

Chapter 6

Discovery of NEED is more important than any other step in the sales cycle – get it right by asking the <u>right</u> questions.

The ability to ask questions is probably the single most dominant factor for business success. The only way to learn what the other person really needs is to ask questions. According to a Harvard Business review in 2017, the single most common reason for the lack of success in selling is that salespeople fail to listen to the customer's needs and start selling too quickly. That's called shooting from the lip.

The entire sales process should start by establishing the business needs in order to understand WHY the customer is looking to invest. What challenges exist today? What are the implications of those challenges?

While planning for a customer meeting, start your questioning preparation by thinking about the four different types of questions:

- **Verification**
- **Need Identification**
- **Opinion**
- **Commitment**

These are four distinctly different types of questions to help you plan a world-class sales meeting that will ensure the maximum progress for everyone involved – you and your customers.

Let's start with the Verification questions. Asking this type of question is an excellent way to start any sales meeting. They allow you to confirm the agenda, the duration of the meeting, and most importantly, the **customer's** objectives for the meetings. **By way of examples ...**

- **Can I just verify the objectives we discussed earlier for this meeting?**

- **Can I confirm we still have an hour for today's meeting?**

- **Are you still looking to make a decision later this month?**

The next type of questions – Need Identification – focuses on the crucial aspect of establishing the real business needs. This is probably the heart of good selling and an area that too many salespeople overlook.   Sometimes, the customer may think they need more storage or servers, but there may be a better solution – software or services, for example, that will drive greater cost reduction or revenue improvement.

Start the process by mulling over all the Need Identification questions you need to ask at the **FACTUAL LEVEL.** This may include asking about the existing IT infrastructure, how many people there are in a particular department, how long it takes to recover critical data, and so on.

These are what we call first-level or factual questions in the Need Identification process.   They are just the **tip of the iceberg** in terms of creating or uncovering business needs.

The second level looks at seeking out the **PROBLEMS** or **CHALLENGES** that the customer may be experiencing within the current infrastructure.

We need to **think like doctors**, that is, we need to uncover the true pain and not diagnose too quickly, just because we hear what we THINK is a need. When you visit a doctor, you hope he or she will get to the root cause of your pain and ONLY THEN prescribe the right course of treatment. It's similar in selling – without the ability to uncover needs, we are left with only a response to requirements that may not be in the best interests of the customer.

The process needs to continue to establish the **IMPLICATION or CONSEQUENCE** of the customer's statements. These are the most important questions and will help establish the **real** cause of the problems and challenges.

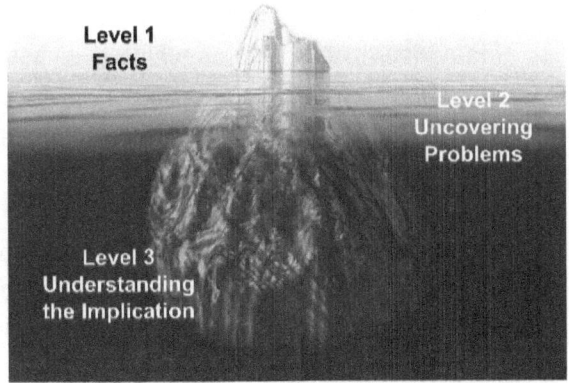

By way of examples ...

- "What do you see as the main business objectives for the new project?" (NEW INFORMATION – level 1)

- "What improvements would you like to see in the overall customer experience?" (NEW INFORMATION – level 2)

- "You have said that you would like to create a serious differentiation in your service levels – what is the implication if this is not achieved? (NEW INFORMATION - level 3)

Now, complete the picture with the last two types – our third type of question are OPINION based – aimed at establishing how the customer views your ideas and suggestions. These are quite easy!

"What are your thoughts on the ideas?" An OPINION question is aimed at uncovering the customer's views – a chance to gain feedback on how well you are doing. Don't take the risk of leaving without first checking the customer's perceptions. It's easy to ask but not so easy to find out a week from now that the customer never had any intentions of pursuing your ideas!

End the process with a COMMITMENT question aimed to ensure that the customer is really on board! **"Would you be willing to introduce us to the Finance Manager to discuss…?"**

Chapter 7

The Power of Silence and Great Listening

Are you a good listener or someone who is just waiting to speak?

How good of a listener are you? Before you respond, think about this. According to the Forrester annual Executive Buyer Study, eight out of ten buyers believe that agendas are driven by the seller's perspective rather than theirs, and one third believe that the seller is only listening for a key word or two, so that they can launch into their sales pitch.

Sobering insight! Here are a few guidelines for being an effective listener.

1. **Encourage silence to show that you are actively listening.** Many salespeople only wait a split second before responding to a customer's comments or questions. Instead, develop the habit of waiting for a minimum of three to four seconds before responding. Even count to yourself to ensure that enough time elapses. This conscious pause will make the person feel heard and comfortable enough to talk more, since your pause demonstrates that you have a sincere interest in what they are saying.
Although many salespeople find the conscious effort to stay quiet challenging, silence creates the space that will motivate your customer to share additional information with you. It also gives you enough time to respond thoughtfully and intelligently to your

customer's specific needs.

2. **Never interrupt the customer while he/she is speaking.** Obviously, what we were taught as children still applies. Enough said.

3. **Be present.** Listen with an open mind (without filters or judgment). Focus on what the customer is saying (or trying to say) instead of being overly concerned with closing a sale. This shows that you have a genuine interest in helping them, not just yourself. Otherwise, you run the risk of missing the subtle nuances or inferences that could make or stall the sale. Maintain eye contact and take down relevant notes to show you are listening.

4. **Make the customer feel heard.** This goes beyond simply becoming a better listener. It involves ensuring that the person whom you are listening to actually feels heard. In order to make someone feel heard, clarify what the customer has said during the conversation. Rephrase their comments or questions in your own words to ensure that you not only heard but understood them. If you need more information for greater context and a fuller picture, a clarifier can sound like the following:

    - "For my own understanding, what you are saying is …"
    - "To further clarify this …"
    - "What I am hearing is …"

5. **Resist the temptation to rebut.** As human beings, we have a natural tendency to resist any new information that conflicts with what we personally believe.   Often, when we hear someone saying something that we might disagree with, we immediately begin building a rebuttal in our mind to obliterate the message that we are receiving.   And if we are focused on creating a rebuttal, we are not listening.   Remember, you can always rebut later.   After you have heard the whole message and had the time to think about it.

6. **Listen for information.**   Consider that during most conversations with customers, we listen **to** information. In other words, we only hear their words. However, when you listen **for** information, you are looking under the words to explore the implied meaning.   This prevents you from wrongly prejudging or misinterpreting the message that the customer is attempting to communicate.   There are four main things we listen for when speaking with a customer:

Listening is a learned and practiced skill, which will open up new selling opportunities that you may never have noticed. It allows you to receive and process valuable information that may have been missed or neglected otherwise.   So, invest the time needed to sharpen your listening skills. Have a family or friend read you a page from a book or newspaper and then paraphrase what you have heard. Take notes as you listen.

Chapter 8

The Essential Art of NUTCASE Qualification

If you do not qualify from the first to the last customer meeting, you are failing to sell effectively. The selling time is precious time, and you need to optimize this time efficiently. The effective qualification of a prospect is a skill that we believe should be covered in the first training session for every individual starting on a sales job. It's a skill set that may feel slightly intrusive at first but is one that saves everyone's time Good qualification ensures all your activities will impact revenue and reveal the problems in each opportunity, so you can plan all subsequent steps accordingly.

You need to eliminate surprises in selling and sell in a controlled and intentional manner.

So, what do you think is the biggest waste of a salesperson's time? Internal meetings? Travel time? Expenses? Well, it's none of these! The biggest waste of a salesperson's time is spending time on a deal and then losing it. How do we avoid that trap or, at the very least, reduce the risk?

Have you ever reached the end of your sales campaign, sent a proposal, and then wondered why the prospect went silent on you? It's probably because you didn't qualify your prospect properly. Think about a recent prospect that disappeared from the radar for no apparent reason and read the rest of this section with that prospect in mind ...

Think NUTCASE.

NUTCASE is an acronym with each letter covering an element of the qualification process. It takes a couple of minutes to complete but could save you loads of time.

Each area of the template should be answered honestly (you cannot kid yourself) and rated with a score from 1 to 5, 1 being "poor understanding" and 5 being "complete understanding". The maximum score therefore is 35. (7 rows with maximum of 5 per row.)

Each time you attend a meeting the score should progress, and if it doesn't, then it may be one of those meetings that resulted in little, no, or negative feedback that you read about in Chapter 1.

NUTCASE Qualification

Salesperson:				Date:		
Account:				Anticipated close date:		

Customer/Prospect:	1	2	3	4	5	Total
N – NEEDS • Do we fully understand the customer's objectives for this project? • Are there further needs we could identify? • How will success be measured in business terms?						
U – UNIQUES • Have we differentiated our offering? • Do we have an overwhelming advantage? • How can we link our uniques to specific business outcomes?						
T – TIMESCALES • Do we understand the timescales and more importantly why they have been set?						
C – CASH: Investment • Do you fully understand the investment level? • What is the ROI and payback?						
A – AUTHORITY • Are we talking to the decision maker? • Are we in direct contact with a sponsor that recognizes the need to act?						
S – SOLUTION • Have we considered every product/service/solution to meet the customer's business objectives? • Are there additional services we should consider? • Is the customer looking at creative financial solutions?						
E – ENEMIES • Do we know who we are competing against? • Do they have any major advantages over us? • How can we position greater value?						
					TOTAL	

N.B. Key to scale.
If your understanding/knowledge/information is:
Poor tick 1. Minimal tick 2. Needing confirmation tick 3. Mostly confirmed tick 4. Complete tick 5.

<u>Remember, Where There Are Low Scores, You Need To Check Each Point Without Delay!</u>

- The process starts with **"N"** for **NEEDS**. As you've already heard many times, establishing the needs before ever starting to present a product or service is the number one objective for EVERY sale. Consider a deal you are working on right now and ask yourself if you have a real strong understanding of the business, IT, and any other needs. If not, build your questions and head back to your customer. Be honest with yourself.

- The **"U"** asks you to consider the **UNIQUE** aspects of your solution. Have you outlined why your solution is better than any alternative? What will your solution deliver that no other can? Score yourself again and, if the rating is low, go back to your team and start thinking about the answer. Be creative and think outside the box.

- The **"T"** in **NUTCASE** questions you regarding the customer's **TIMESCALES** for this project. Do you know what they are? Have you determined why a particular day or month has been chosen? What is the implication if this is not achieved?

- **"C"** is for **CASH** or **investment level.** Stop asking for the budget and start asking about the customer's planned INVESTMENT level. It sends out a different message. Where there is investment, it suggests that there should be a return on that investment. Enquire about how the customer will fund the project? Are there creative financing options that you could offer that spread the cost and avoid large capital expenditure? And most importantly, consider how you can build the business case in order to demonstrate how your solution will drive the maximum return on the investment. Score yourself on the scale of 1-5.

- The **"A"** in **NUTCASE** refers to **AUTHORITY.** Are you certain you are talking to the right people, who can truly make the final decision? If you are talking to Procurement, who is the person in the organization who will ultimately benefit from your solution? Be honest as your score this one.

- Which brings us to the **"S" – SOLUTION.** Have you considered every aspect of your proposed solution? Are you merely responding to what the customer says they want? Can there be additional services or products that deliver even greater returns for the customer? Score yourself on the 1-5 scale.

- Finally, we have the **"E"** standing for **ENEMIES.** This refers to your competition, which could be external or internal. In other words, do you know who you are up against? Have you asked the question of multiple people in the buying organization? Is this a competitor you know, and if so, what do you think their strategy will be? How can you ensure and demonstrate even greater business outcomes? Is it feasible that the customer could go with an internal fix for the requirement? Keep asking pertinent questions but avoid interrogating the customer!

You should now be able to arrive at a score between 0 and 35. If the sale is predicted to close within 4 weeks and the score is below 20, you may want to go back and re-check every element of the NUTCASE tool.

Effective Sales Qualification requires a constant, inquisitive state of mind, where you are discovering and validating with questions throughout the opportunity. It makes for pretty uncomfortable reading, but CSO Insights' latest global study of sales forecasting accuracy suggests that, on a deal-by-deal basis, it is close to an all-time low at 46.5%. To put that in context, simply tossing a coin will provide more accurate results.

The consequences are equally unpleasant: forecasts are missed, and personal credibility diminished. Here are a few final reminders:

1. Qualification isn't an event; it's a continuous process.
2. Re-qualify at every stage; constantly recheck and re-qualify factors that have previously "passed the test."
3. Measure progress based on outcomes – in terms of what your prospect has done or said (Use the "Opinion" questions at every opportunity to check your progress from the perspective of each influencer).
4. Top performers qualify differently – they qualify out unless there is sound evidence to the contrary.
5. Sales management plays a critical role in helping salespeople justify why their deals should remain in the pipeline.

Chapter 9

Handling Objections and Closing Your Calls

You are almost certain to encounter obstacles on your way to making a sale!   Treat them positively!   Exhibit that you are capable of listening, understanding, and sharing in them.
The Guidelines for that are as follows:

- CHECK your understanding.
- LISTEN to the objection.
- PAUSE before replying.   Give yourself the time to think, time for the prospect to qualify the objection, or even to answer it themselves!
- EMPTY THE BUCKET.   Question the relevant people to uncover any remaining objections or use a trial close.
- RESPOND CONFIDENTLY!   Don't bluff your way out.
- CONFIRM that the objection has been resolved.
- CAPITALISE!   This may be an opportunity to seek some form of commitment.

Demands for Concessions
Remember the first rule of negotiation.   "If you don't have to bargain, don't do it."   A 10% discount may wipe 50% of the profit margin.   Defend your price to the hilt.   Try to establish that yours is the preferred solution; sell the value of a better service, better performance, higher quality, etc.

Closing Your Calls
Successful selling largely concerns making it easy for the prospects to buy.   The more help you offer them in the

difficult process of making the buying decision, the greater is the likelihood that they'll look to you for help in the implementation process. The closing stages of a call represent a golden opportunity for you to demonstrate the professional touch.

Close your calls with these objectives in mind:

Check the achievement of call objectives
- The prospect will be reassured that the time spent on the call was time well spent. Whilst, from your viewpoint, you will get the confirmation that you have passed another milestone in your sales campaign, leading to a logical progression to the next one.

Eliminate Misunderstanding
- Check that both you and the prospect share the same understanding pertaining to the key issues.

Underline Your Professionalism
- Just by going through the SUMMARY process, you quietly add great value to your credibility as a professional!

End of Call Summary Techniques
- Summarize the key points of your discussion.
- Make your summary accurate, complete, and concise.
- Confirm that the prospect is in agreement.
- Use phrases such as "Am I right?"," Do you see it that way?", and "I think we agreed that..."
- Get involvement and commitment from the prospect
- Create future joint activities.

- Set a realistic TARGET action that you will ask the customer to undertake after each meeting.
- Use the trial close: "If we can.... Will you?"

REMEMBER TO CONFIRM ALL THE KEY POINTS AND ACTIONS THROUGH EMAIL.

Chapter 10

"BODY TALK"

Your image at work is the way you appear to others. Even if you feel you do not have a particular image, other people will have formed an impression of you and your personality, and this applies to both those who you know well and those you have just met!   It is impossible NOT to communicate ideas about yourself.

Difficulties and misunderstandings arise when you are unaware of the impression you are giving off or when you think you come across a certain way, whereas you are perceived quite differently.

You can control your behaviour, so that you give out only the messages you want to give.   It is not an exact science and is always open to different interpretations, but you can minimize the possibility of giving a false impression of yourself.

What body language will not do for you
Do not simply assume that knowing about body language is a sure-shot route to fooling others regarding your real personality, abilities. and intentions or that you will be able to read other people's minds.

Although non-verbal behaviour can be learnt and controlled, this does not guarantee that you will be able to hide certain discrepancies between your real feelings and the impression you wish to create. Our communicative behaviour is subject to *leakage*. This term refers to the unconscious signals we emit that leak out information about our real feelings and attitudes. Slight physical gestures that you are unaware of can reveal emotional states, such as anger, tension, or nervousness.

Tapping your fingers or feet, rapid blinking, fiddling with a tie or jewellery may communicate messages that contradict your words. These micro-gestures are overcome in a flash, but if they are picked up, they can offer an insight into what is going on behind the surface impression. When we speak of having a sixth sense or a hunch about someone, quite often the fact is that we have sub-consciously recognized and responded to these very signals.

When our outward gestures match our words and our intentions, we display *congruence*. This means that everything fits together and that there are no contradictions in our communication.

Achieving congruence
The closer the match between your inner state and your behaviour, the more convincing your body language signals will be. Having a positive self-image is crucial to manage the impression that you have of yourself and that you convey to others. If you see yourself in a negative light, your body language will convey a lack of confidence and self-esteem. A vicious circle is then set up as others respond to your low self-value. A way to break this cycle and manage a positive impression of yourself is to act

yourself into a particular state of mind. Your mind will actually follow your body. For example, if you want to feel lively and energetic, think about how your body behaves when you are feeling that way. Remember how you stand and walk, your facial expression, how you move your head. Once you have mentally tuned into your body's pattern, imbibe it physically. Follow your body's natural pattern, behave as you usually do when in an energetic frame of mind, and you will access the same energized feeling. (Incidentally, this is a great way to get yourself out of a slump at work). So, if you want to be seen as an authoritarian figure, learn and use body language that conveys authority and you will strengthen your self-confidence.

The way you behave influences the way that you feel, and the way other people behave towards you, which, in turn, affects the way you feel about yourself. The vicious circle can then become a circle of confidence.

Standing Tall
Your posture and the way that you stand and walk provides some insight into your personality and state of mind. During conversations and interactions with others, your posture will change as you respond and adjust to different people and situations, but you probably have a distinctive, habitual way of standing and walking. You may slouch or hunch your shoulders – all the positions that could be seen as depicting a lack of confidence. An upright, balanced posture sends a positive message.

People who stand and move with their head raised and

their shoulders squared convey a sense of self-esteem and confidence.

Facial expression
What is your facial expression when it is in repose, that is, while you are not interacting with someone or reacting to a situation?   Your habitual expression may be a slight frown or a turned down mouth.   People will assume you have personal characteristics associated with that facial expression.   Without being aware of it, you may come across as grumpy or worried.   Or aloof and haughty.   Your facial expression is the first thing people notice about you.

The power of a smile
Everyone responds positively to a smile.   If you smile when you greet people, you indicate a willingness to be pleasant and communicate.   And your smile is likely to be returned.   False smiles are revealed through other signals.   When we smile genuinely, our eyes wrinkle a little at the edges and our mouth curves spontaneously.   Disingenuous smiles do not reach the eyes, and the mouth can look fixed or twisted.

Achieving a powerful public face
Imagine that you just caught sight of someone you are pleased to see.   What expression does your face assume?   Relaxed? Open?   Friendly?   With your eyes a little wide and your mouth slightly upturned?   Practice getting it right.   You may have to use your facial muscles to unfurrow your brow, to lift your eyebrows, and to stop

your mouth from turning down.

The language of clothes
The way you dress makes a statement about who you are. Whatever may be your reasons for wearing clothes, other people will interpret your appearance and draw conclusions about various characteristics of you, ranging from what kind of a job you do to what kind of a personality you have.

Dress for success
The advice that is often given is to dress for the job you want, not for the job you have. Use your judgement to ascertain how far this practice will help you climb the professional ladder! Use your judgement for how any attempt to stand out from the crowd will be perceived. You may feel that your cartoon tie or scarf shows you have a fun personality, but others may not see it in the same way.

Shaking hands
One of the origins of the handshake is said to be the gesture our ancestors exchanged when they wanted to prove that they were not carrying a weapon. There is no threat or anxiety when someone can see your open palm. We form an impression of someone by the way they shake hands.

A firm handshake (but not bone crushing, since this may depict dominance or aggression) is thought to be a sign of strength and honesty, especially when accompanied by a warm smile and steady eye contact.

A weak handshake or, say, one in which only the fingertips make contact may be seen as an indication of ineffectiveness and negativity. A damp palm could be read as nervousness. However, be careful to not use the handshake as the basis of your judgement of someone.

Eye contact
The general pattern is that people in conversation look at each other for 30–60% of the time. Any longer than that can be seen as unsettling, embarrassing, or threatening. Eye contact of lesser frequency is interpreted as indicating qualities, such as insincerity or lack of interest.

Judging the right amount of visual contact is a matter of skill and practice. Looking at the person whom you are speaking to is vital to build strong communication and rapport. Try to hold the person's gaze for a few seconds before glancing away, then make your next eye contact last a little longer.

As a listener, it can be difficult to maintain visual contact without the look becoming a fixed stare. Try to focus your gaze on the upper part of the face and remember to respond with head and facial movements. Your eyes will shift as you respond, creasing as you smile or opening up wide as you show surprise or interest. Not only does this demonstrate that you are paying attention, but it will also help you feel and appear more natural.

Open and closed body language

A characteristic of effective body language is its openness. By keeping your gestures AWAY from your body, you indicate that you have nothing to hide.

If you fold your arms, you create a BARRIER, and this could be seen as a defensive stance. Your arms form a protective guard in front of you. This is the position that we sometimes assume when we disagree with what is being said and are not going to budge from our point of view!

Sometimes we adopt a modified version of this gesture by putting one arm across the body – a position that can be seen to indicate nervousness or the lack of self-confidence. A barrier can also be created if our hands are held high in front of us, with the fingers intertwined. This implies a negative or defensive attitude.

Listening

The most important thing is to show that you are listening. Listening must not only take place but also be seen to take place.

Respond by giving little nods to show that you are taking an active interest in what is being said. Listen to the whole message and use the summary technique to check your understanding.

A low-pitched voice can give the impression of authority and control, whereas if your natural pitch is high, you may come across as lightweight or emotional.

About the Author

Sue Aspinall is a highly experienced sales professional, with over 15 years of account and sales management experience in the IT industry. Sue and Tony Ellis (the former founder of Exceed) saw a gap in the market in the mid-90s to help sales team members transform their overall approach to one based on recognizing that successful selling and consistent results are achieved by demonstrating quantified business value to customers. This, supported by best practices of healthy and disciplined sales management, is the way to drive higher margins, reduce the average sales-cycle time, and avoid being locked in a price and product centric discussion with customers. Sue has a passion for helping salespeople achieve long-term success and change their sales behaviours. She frequently guides sales teams on strategies to win new and extension business and is paid and measured against the success achieved.

About Exceed

Since 1990, Exceed has worked with more than 500 organizations to drive significant revenue, margin, and market share for our clients. Exceed transforms the language of selling from price and product to quantified business value – we believe that selling is about showing customers how to make money, save money, or do both.

Every Consulting Team Member has a minimum of 15 years of sales and sales management experience, meaning that we understand and empathize with our audiences.

Our uniqueness lies in the fact that we link your value proposition with Exceed's business value selling methodologies, showing sales team members not only WHAT to sell but also more importantly HOW to sell these solutions in the most effective way, that is, with a business case that demonstrates the tangible value your customers expect to achieve as a result of making any investment in your services and solutions.

Sales Managers are critical to the success of a sales transformation program and Exceed offers various programs to equip these team members with the skills and tools necessary to lead and coach their teams, ensuring a tight control over the pipeline and the introduction of healthy and disciplined best sales practices to reduce the sales cycle and the maximum margin.

The Exceed Deal-Planning Methodology ensures a tight control over every key sales opportunity, resulting in a positive and long-term impact on the win-to-loss ratio. When an increase in share of wallet in a key account is required, we engage with industry experts to identify the real challenges the customer is facing. Then, we build a proactive plan to demonstrate the value your organization can bring to the customer's table.

In many cases, we practice what we preach, offering our clients a risk and reward engagement model, whereby we link our fees to your success.

Contact Exceed-Global
www.exceed-global.com - +44 1925 755759

Sales Meeting Planner

Account:	Completed by:		Call Date:

Customer(s)	Title	Customer(s)	Title

Your Meeting Objectives (SMART & try to set a minimum of 3)

1. 2.

3. 4.

Compelling Business Reason for the meeting (from the Customer's point of view)

Key Questions

Verification	New Information (NB: Probe for the consequence or implication of any problem)
Opinion	Commitment

Best Action Commitment

Minimum Acceptable Action

Opening Statement

Possible Objections	Counters

Don't forget to practice Golden Silence I and II

w to stand out from the crowd ...

It's a buyer's market.   Anyone engaged in sales can tell you that.   As a result, a lot of salespeople are stuck in unproductive sales cycles, in which they sell against competitors, feature by feature, in a cost-driven process.   Now, that's a strategy designed for failure.   If you are the low-cost leader today, someone else will replace you tomorrow.   And, if the features you offer are unique, they won't be for long.   In today's hyper-competitive environment, successful features spread faster than viruses.

To negotiate and close profitable sales deals today, you must change the way you think about what you offer and who you target within a prospect's organization.   And if you believe you can do this based on the strength of your account relationships, you're going to be disappointed.

Selling is both a science and an art – follow the rules (the science) and make it look like an art.   This book sets out practical and easy to implement techniques and skills that make a great difference once they become part of a salesperson's muscle memory.

www.ingramcontent.com/pod-product-compliance
Lightning Source LLC
Chambersburg PA
CBHW030513220526
45464CB00006B/2773